STACKPOLE STAINED GLASS PATTERNS

Birds of the Beach

T0346199

STACKPOLE STAINED GLASS PATTERNS

Birds of the Beach

STACKPOLE
BOOKS

Published by
STACKPOLE BOOKS
5067 Ritter Road
Mechanicsburg, PA 17055
www.stackpolebooks.com

Printed in the United States of America

10 9 8 7 6 5 4 3 2 1

First edition

ISBN 978-0-8117-1471-6

Selecting Glass

The birds in these patterns represent common species found on the beach or near the ocean. The accompanying color illustrations offer suggestions is to what colors of glass might be used for the projects. Many of these birds have subtle patterns that can be wonderfully represented with streaky, multicolored, and mottled glass—especially wispy whites, browns, grays, and golds. These birds are, in general, more colorful and striking in their breeding plumages. Consult a bird identification guide or color photographs to help you choose the glass that matches what you see. Have fun!

Using the Patterns

Since many birds of the beach are rather large, you'll likely want to use these patterns at an enlarged size. Set a copier at 120 or 130 percent and see if you like what you get. To display the pieces, you can simply solder loops for hanging to the top of the panel; you can also frame the panels in lead or wooden stained glass frames (available at a stained glass shop). And you can easily add surrounding pieces to the patterns to create larger panels that have the dimensions you want.

Creating Eyes

Some of these patterns include eyes. To create the eyes, nip out a small gap in the glass along the appropriate edges and fill the gap with solder. Or you can cut and foil a tiny circle of glass to fill in the gap. Another way to create eyes is to paint them directly on the glass (using paints made especially for glass). If you do this, make sure the glass is clean and dry before you paint.

Herring Gull #1

Semipalmated Plover

Semipalmated Plover

Atlantic Puffin

Common Tern

Common Tern

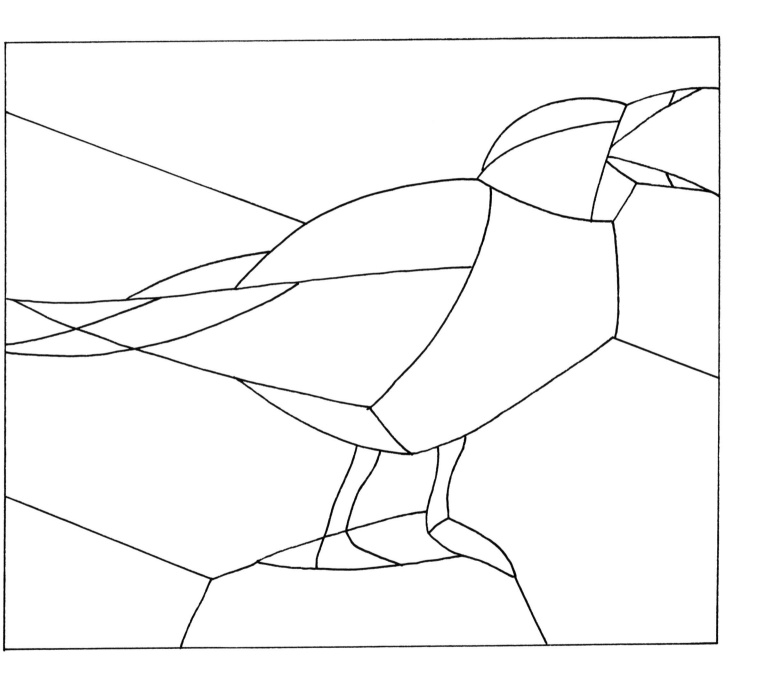

Least Sandpiper

Herring Gull #2

Herring Gull #2

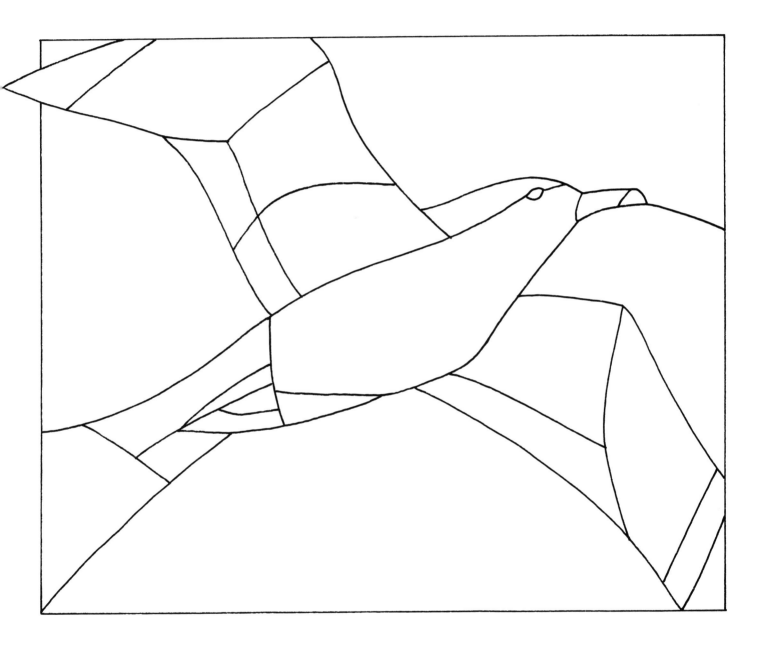

Dunlin

Dunlin

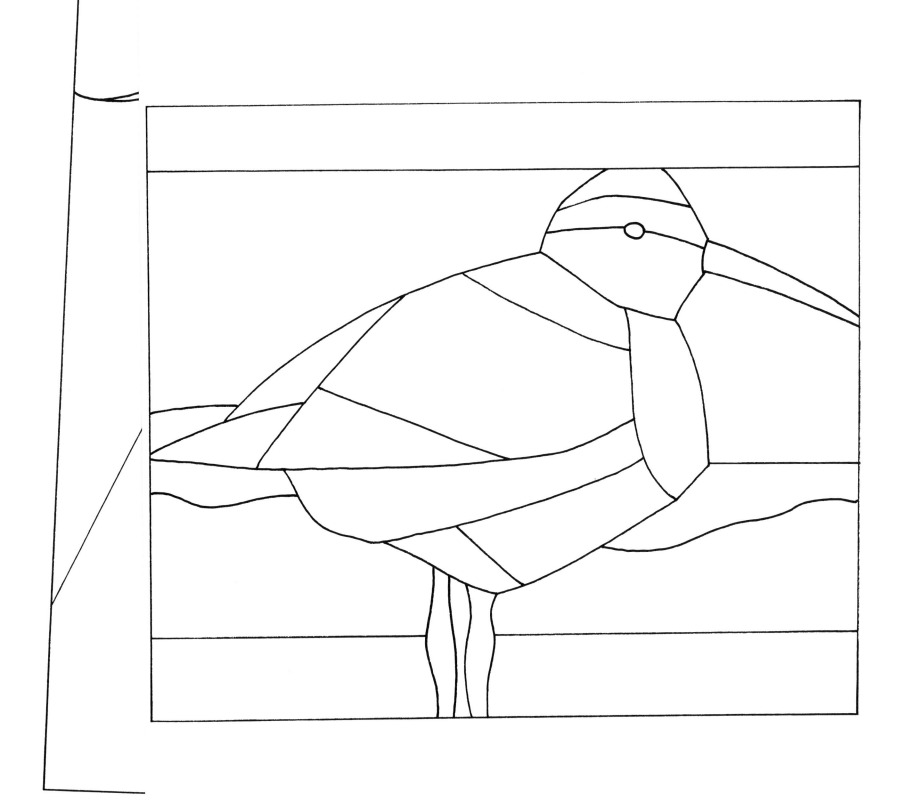

Red Knot

Red Knot

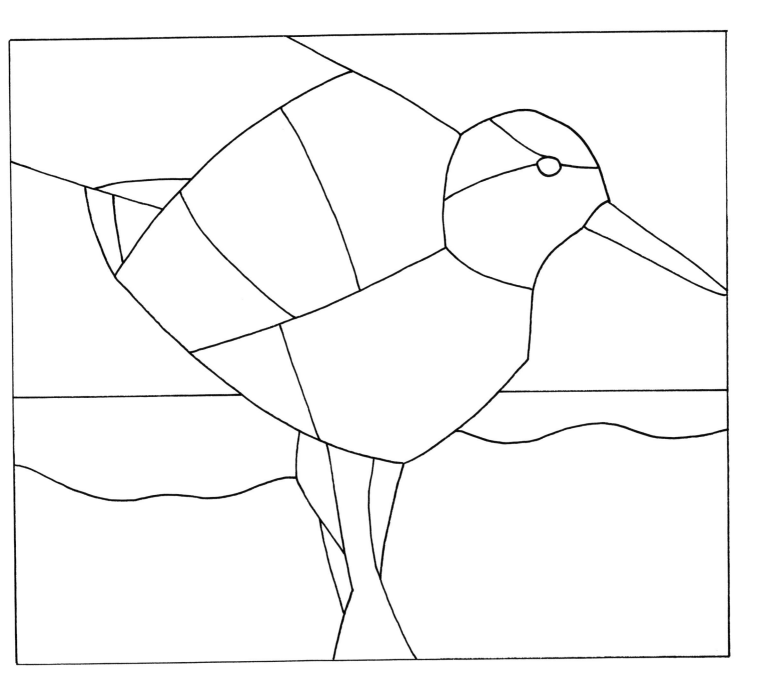

Laughing Gull

Laughing Gull

Brown Pelican

Brown Pelican

Black-bellied Plover

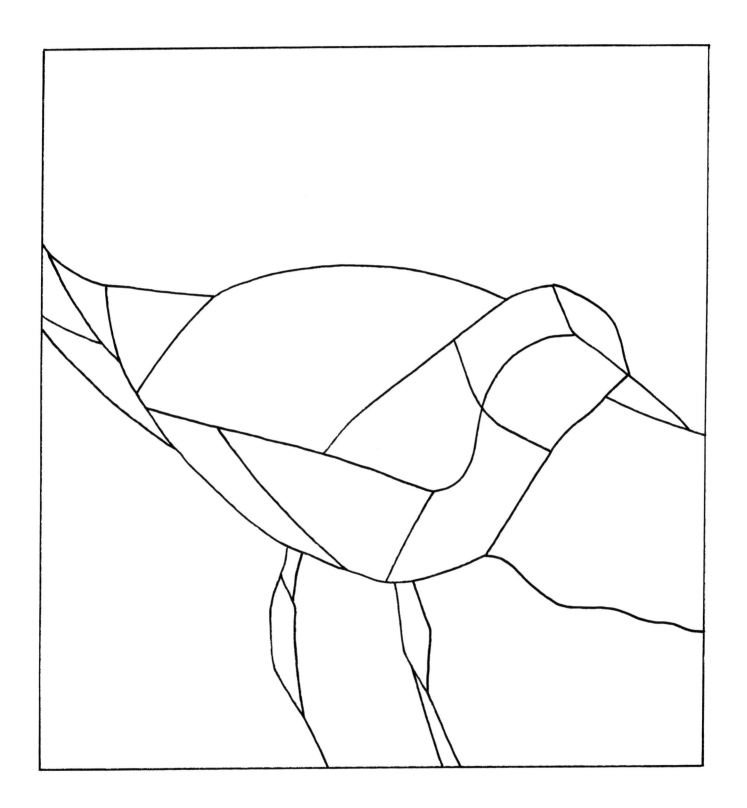

Piping Plover

Piping Plover

Spotted Sandpiper

Spotted Sandpiper

Common Terns

Common Terns

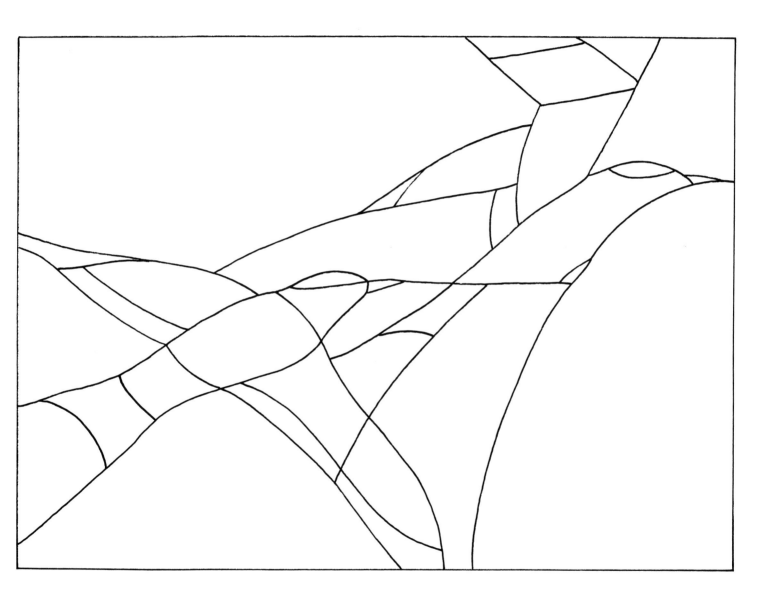

Common Loon

Common Loon

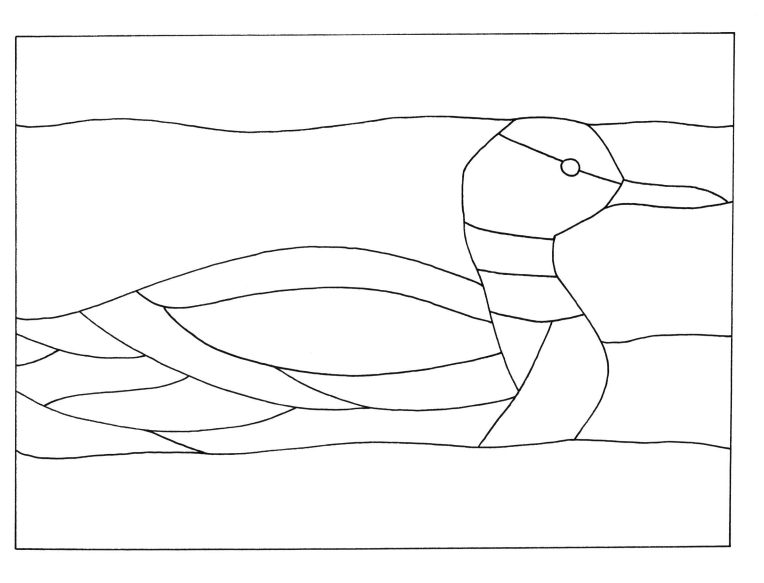

Blue-footed Booby

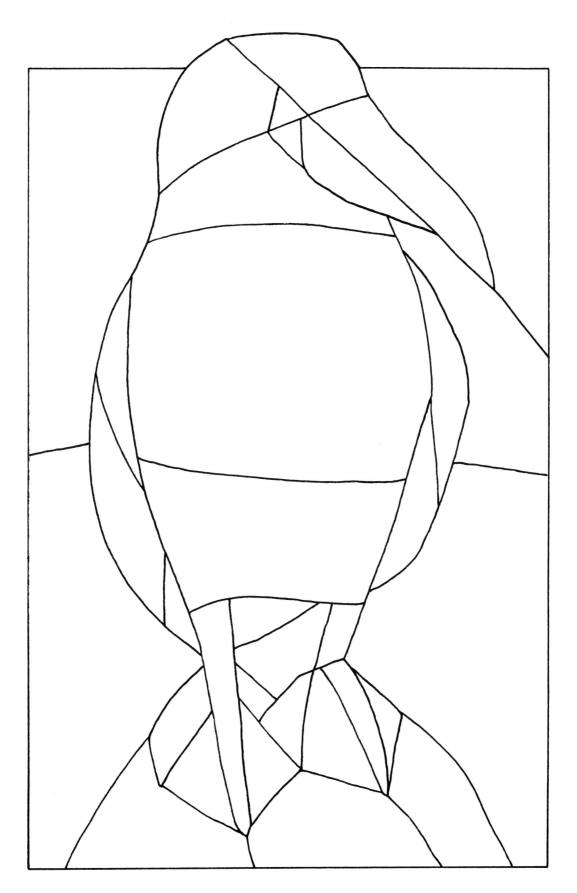

Black-necked Stilt

Black-necked Stilt

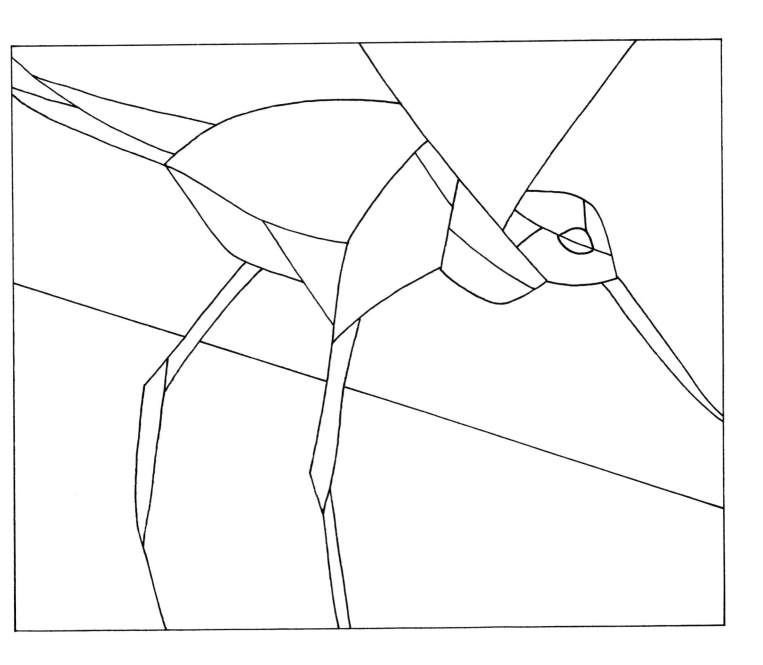

Willet

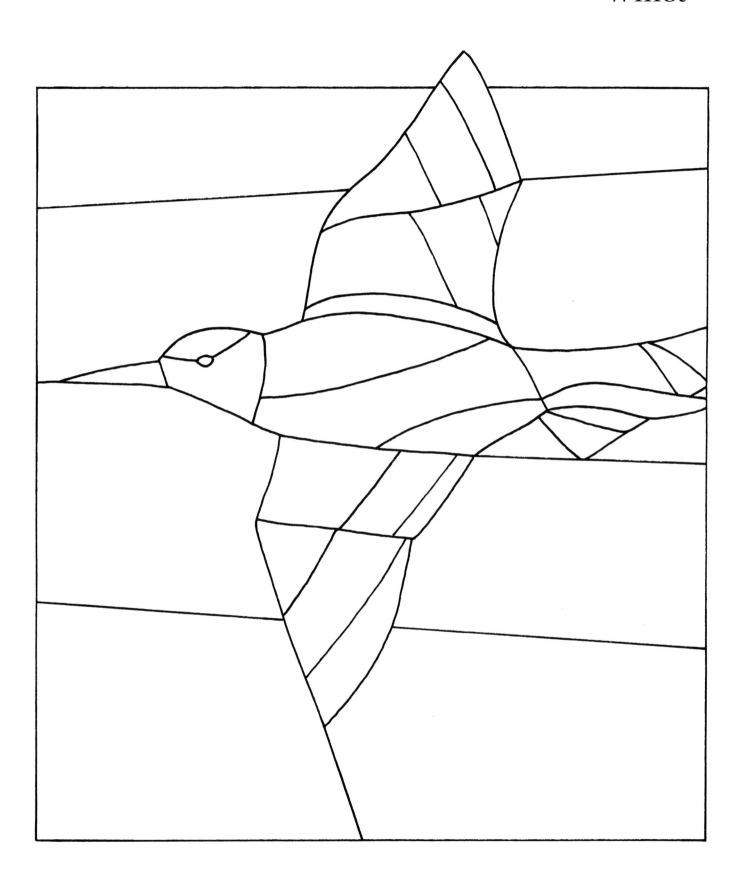

Sanderling

Sanderling

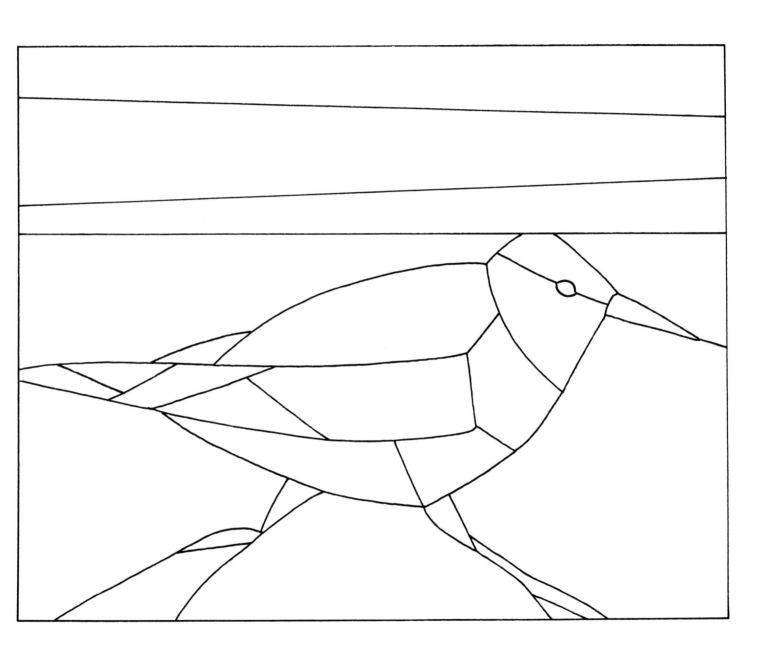

Also Available in the
STACKPOLE STAINED GLASS PATTERNS SERIES

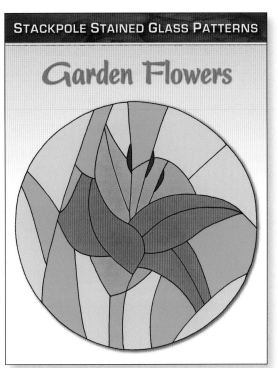

BEAUTIFUL LEAVES
978-0-8117-1341-2

GARDEN FLOWERS
978-0-8117-1344-3

WWW.STACKPOLEBOOKS.COM
1-800-732-3669

Also Available in the
STACKPOLE STAINED GLASS PATTERNS SERIES

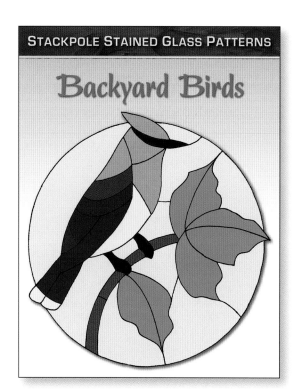

BACKYARD BIRDS
978-0-8117-1342-9

SONGBIRDS
978-0-8117-1343-6

WWW.STACKPOLEBOOKS.COM
1-800-732-3669